Bumfuzzle

Roberta, Frank, Ordinary Joe and 48
other bittersweet poems about
love, loss and lamb bhuna

Keith Wilson

Bumfuzzle

Roberta, Frank, Ordinary Joe and 48 other bittersweet poems about love, loss and lamb bhuna

Written by Keith Wilson

Cover design by Simon Armstrong

Proofreader: Phil Taylor

Publisher: Fiona Shaw

Printed and bound in Spain by Graficas

ISBN: 978-0-9576945-2-1

First published in November 2013 by Wordscapes
Metal @ Edge Hill Station
Tunnel Road, Liverpool L7 6ND
www.wordscape.org.uk

Foreword

I was first introduced to Keith Wilson by my then-producer Steve Coleman. I have not spoken to Steve since.

As research for this foreword and to uncover any of Keith's unheralded achievements I may have overlooked, I had a look at the varied information available on the World Wide Web. Amongst his unending list of triumphs in the fields of pop and rock music, writing for film and television, directing on stage and screen, numerous acting credits, albums and recordings, mentoring, appearances with giants of the music industry, TV presenting and leading the punk and new wave movement etc. etc., one thing stands out – I'm not mentioned anywhere!!

Keith is indeed a man of many parts, although most of them are now loose and falling off. I can remember listening to one of his early albums and regretting my inability to play some of this great stuff – mainly because BBC standards are much higher than mine.

On reading Keith's first book *Irritable Vowel Syndrome*, the quality and sheer difference in his work was immediately apparent, and he was invited to become a regular on my show. Despite my non-appearance in any of his biographies (and the complete lack of appreciation I have been shown for my integral part in his rise to unheard-of financial and literary success), I have to admit that his slots quickly became one of the highlights in my show – even taking over from the mega-popular travel bulletins.

When the shop at BBC Radio Merseyside began stocking Keith's book, the response was amazing. As soon as copies were delivered, they both sold out. Within a month, queues of one formed as news of more stocks filtered through.

So what is Keith's appeal? Well, meet him, read his books or listen to his CDs, and you'll find a wordsmith who can juggle nouns, adjectives and verbs with the skill of a circus genius. A man who could be rightly placed amongst the icons of '60s Liverpool poets Adrien Henri, Roger McGough and Brian Patten.

I describe him as ‘the poet with the punch line’. His skill at introducing a killer last line is poetry and comedy writing at its best. His words invoke both passion and humour. In short, he is a master of his craft.

Billy Butler
BBC Radio Merseyside

SHE

Although slightly larger
Than her Facebook page suggested
The compensation was more than fair
She was gloriously full-chested
Amongst the slender, sleek and painfully thin
Skeletal saints and thinners
She'd plainly had more meat pies
Than I've had hot dinners
But in this bleached teeth, siliconed
Disneyfied modern world
It's an uplifting and refreshing change
To find an un-enhanced girl

She was Rubenesque, voluptuous
Fleshy and well-rounded
Her ability to burp the alphabet
Left onlookers astounded
She had that mischievous twinkle
In those sparkling eyes of blue
Especially the left one
The straighter of the two
And although her raucous flatulence
Could set off car alarms

In slightly less than no time at all
I was spellbound by her charms

She was an eyeball pleaser
I wanted to squeeze her
She was ten degrees cooler
Than a polar bear's freezer
She juggled pickled eggs
And drank snake bites
And kept a saucerful of secrets
In the gusset of her tights

She was differently charmed and finely tuned
Like some Gothic Cinderella
So you can imagine the shock when she told me
She used to be a fella

My head was thrown into disarray
Disorganised, chaotic, shambolic
And that's why I'm here – my name's Keith
And I'm an alcoholic

NETHER WALLOP

I woke up in a sweat with my eyebrows singed
And both feet in my pyjama jacket sleeve
My back to front vest was torn and ragged
My underpants hard to believe
Forty shades of grey with a burnt ochre trim
And scorch mark decorations on each leg
They were stuck to the headboard with what looked
    like hoisin sauce
And a half exploded Cadbury's Cream Egg

There were no legs left on the king size bed
Not a finger on the alarmed clock
The wardrobe door was on the window ledge
With a shoe, a trouser leg and a smoking sock

A faint smell of sulphur hung in the air
The windows were cracked and steamed up
Both pillowcases were burning on the lights
And a set of false teeth were in my cup

Evidence of combustion hung about the place
The floor was littered with empty bottles and cans
The television screen was upside down against the door
With the toilet and bathroom extractor fans

My legs were dead and my back was raw
The room looked like a building site
Never again will I take a sleeping pill
And a laxative on the same night

ORDINARY JOE

Ordinary Joe rolled out of bed
Longing for an ordinary day
Went to the bathroom in his slippers
Blew a tune on the Cor Anglais

He pulled a face then a muscle in the mirror
Showered, shivered, shaved and got dressed
And to round off his ordinary ablutions
On the window he drew a deep breath

At the breakfast table Mrs Joe
While picking a fight with the bread
Hurled a Marmite jar into the back yard
Killing a blackbird stone dead

After smashing then trashing the toaster
She kicked a boiled egg down the hall
Stuck the bread knife in the leg of the table
And made an obscene telephone call

Ordinary Joe composed himself
And made his way downstairs
Mrs Joe punched the heating thermostat
And battered a banana and two pears

He smiled as a collander bounced off his head
And ignored the small fire in the sink
And after wiping the baked beans off the
 Venetian blind
He went out into the yard to think

He could still remember her laughter
All those good times they'd shared in the past
And not for the first time Joe wondered
Just how long the menopause would last

The House, The Flat
The Dog and the Hat

I've only got myself to blame
And I know how it looks
Family, friends, acquaintances
I've rewritten their bad books

Some people won't even look at me
Relationships have become so strained
My stiff upper lip's now a slack lower jaw
I'm isolated as well as ashamed

At first it was curiosity
But it soon became an addiction
Even the threat of going to jail
Did nothing to arrest the affliction

I borrowed more and more money
Got into more and more debt
Lost the house and flat, the dog and the hat
Became aggressive, confused and upset

I suffered shortness of breath
And outbursts of profanity
Nearly went to jail again
Struggled with my sanity

Wrestled violent mood swings
Severe abdominal pains
Grinding other people's teeth
Constipation strains
Backache, headaches
Increased perspiration
The complete loss of libido
Even the Cheryl Cole fixation

Some people don't really want to stop
They just want it to cause less harm
Others recognise the symptoms
But don't see any cause for alarm

Maybe you've got too much money
Or maybe you've not got enough
But you can lose everything you own and more
And it's worse when times are tough

I've made mistakes, I know where I went wrong
And I know it's nothing more than common sense
But I swear I had no idea before this all kicked in
Monopoly could be so intense

INCOMPATIBILITY

She doesn't like my records
Doesn't like my friends
Can't make a decent cup of tea
Never mind amends

Talks and talks when I'm watching a film
Hoovers during *Match of the Day*
Spends half of her time re-adjusting her bra
And the rest buying shite on eBay

She says that I look like death warmed up
Pale, uninteresting and pasty
This from a woman who's an orange shade of brown
Whose meringues have never been tasty
Who taunts me with Mars Bars
Ridicules me with cake
My critics may be fierce but at least they're real
Her knockers are fake

Orange of face, mahogany of thigh
With the dress sense of Fred Flintstone
She only bothers faking orgasms
So she can have another moan

She buys shoes and handbags every other day
Eats salad on its own as a meal
Loves those tiny, useless little dogs
Thinks fake fur coats are real

As unpleasant as inflamed haemorrhoids
And slippery as an anaconda
Even four pints of Absinthe
Couldn't make the heart grow fonder

I should've known she wasn't Cinderella
When she forced that glass slipper on her trotter
And so, in my defence Your Honour
That's why I shot her

NOT LAST NIGHT

Not last night
But the night before
A thunderclap splintered
The bedroom door
My head turned
Through 360 degrees
My abdomen shifted
On a flutter of unease
The fingers on the clock
Flicked a 'v' at the moon
Pictures on the wall
Threw themselves around the room
Bites and scratches
Pierced my skin
A wave of nausea
Made a fist wherein
Another can of worms
And lizardy things
Spat out forked tongues
And unfurled their wings

I convulsed, threw up
I was cold and unredeemed

I accidentally levitated
Screamed and blasphemed

Glass rained from nowhere
And shattered on the wall
The smoke alarm wailed
Like a banshee in the hall
Patterns from the woodchip
Bled across the floor
And the paint job blistered
On the bedroom door

My eyes rolled another six
All bloodshot and red
My tongue flew in a rage
And licked the back of my head
With the gambling debts and scratch cards
It's my fault I'm messed up and stressed
Along with the house, the car and Gibson Les Paul
I've been repossessed

TALKAHOLIC

She talks and talk and talks and talks
She'll draw blood without drawing breath
Imagine a sack of Columbian marching powder
Snorted by the witches from Macbeth
Multiplied by ten to the power of seven
With an added angry wasp in both ears
Within five minutes your trigger finger's itchy
Well I've had to suffer it for years

She called the Samaritans for a bit of a chat
And was four and a half hours on the phone
Explaining how she went on a ballooning holiday
And put on three and a half stone
Then spoke of her strength and will power
In the face of snack bars and cafés
And explained the success of her gin and tonic diet
When she lost over fourteen days

She'll talk about everything and anything
There's never a gap left to fill
If I could get half a word in edgeways
I'd make up some beans to spill

I haven't said a word since 1999
So I comfort eat for sanity's sake
I used to like to say it with flowers
Now I just think it with cake

She'll talk about the vapours, newspapers
Chippy fly papers, comic capers
Suburban swingers, right wingers
Right mingers, final flingers
Duckers, divers, shirkers, skivers

Fertility issues, toilet tissues
Taboos, tattoos and queues for shoes
Implausibility, insecurity
Increased virility, immaturity
Designer shops, flip-flops, gender reassignment ops

Driving bans, fake tans, dirty hands
Beer cans, white vans, elastic bands
Thrills, spills, cheap espadrilles
Waxing, relaxing, red gas bills
Traffic cones, trombones, Jessie J and Tom Jones

Variety shows, new clothes, bathroom overflows
Tomatoes, dominoes, alarm clock radios

Jockeys, hockey, the economy, inflation
Overdue library books, premature adulation
Thinking, banking, drinking and winking

Wheeling and dealing, faith healing
Stealing, stinking, stalking, Darjeeling
Scandals, Scrabble, psychobabble
Toilet door handles, vandals, Wilfred Brambell,
    scented candles
Fridge freezers, tasers, teasers, double glazers,
    diamond geezers

Mobile phones, gastric bands
Office drones, non-stick pans
Needles, pins, original sins
Taking in trousers, taking out bins
Incontinence pants, road tax, house plants, implants

Embarrassing diseases, rare cheeses
The firmament, the government, the day when hell
    freezes
The tasteless, the lazy, the faceless, the tireless
Football moan-ins on the wind-up wireless
Current trends, virtual friends, the banks, the bends
    and Argos pens

On and on and on she went
Day after month after year
Professional intervention failed miserably
Withdrew and disappeared

So I was left to find a sensitive solution
Once the professionals had walked off the job
Now every passing day she's less and less to say
I've wrapped several yards of gaffa tape round her gob

I BLAME MICHAEL BUBLE

People are talking about me
Their words are burning my ears
Tongues wag and fingers point
It's almost reduced me to tears

Those who deliberately slander
Besmirch and attack my good name
Should read the official accident report
It states clearly that I'm not to blame

I bought Grandma the skydiving gift voucher
For her birthday – a fit and active 99
I thought she could fundraise for the pub darts team
With the experience of a lifetime

Not for a second did I think it would go wrong
They said it was just like falling off a log
Nobody mentioned the possibility of jumping
to her death
And destroying an outside lavatory, three sheep
and a small dog

She fell out with the instructor over a Michael
Bublé song
And they went their separate ways in mid air
She was flicking 'v' signs in his general direction
While hurtling towards the ground unaware
That the parachute had jammed and failed to open
And as she inhaled the exhilaration and
screamed 'Girlpower!'
Like some misguided missile she hit a corrugated
iron roof
Legs-a-kimbo at two hundred miles an hour

Two of the sheep died of shock the following day
Sadly, she was pronounced dead at the scene
Her silken parachute still very much virgo intacta
The porcelain throne smashed to smithereens

What a terrible way to end it all
In a bog astride a rusty crop sprayer
She'll be sorely missed – she was a strong and
feisty woman
And a quite splendid banjo player
Yet people are still talking about me
Their words are burning my ears
And having such a delicate and sensitive disposition
I won't get over this for years and years

P.S For Sale
One Parachute
Sixteen stone breaking strain
Only used once
Never opened
One hardly noticeable stain

TIME TO BUY SOME DONUTS

She thought she was early
But was twenty minutes late
Left me waiting under the clock
Like the previous date
And the four before that
And the very first time we met
I know there's a time for everything
But there's no time for regret
So I thought for a minute
And not a second more
Ran my fingers through her hair
And called time on our rapport
Her little hand grabbed my big hand
And although she was visually top notch
I couldn't condone this kind of behaviour
Not on my watch

SPEED DATING

She kicked off with financial security
Mentioned her love of the arts
Touched on past relationships
And her collection of Volkswagen parts

Quizzed him about his childhood
Discussed his most treasured possessions
Whether or not he wanted kids?
His opinion on manic depression

What were his thoughts on religion?
Did he believe in love at first sight?
Was he a red or was he a blue?
Could he handle himself in a fight?

What did he do with his spare time?
Could he remember his very first crush?
Did he really believe a bird in the hand
Was better than two in the bush?

What was his perfect holiday?
His favourite day of the week?
What did he think of Seasick Steve
And Nigella Lawson's physique?

Where did he see himself in five years' time?
Did he believe in life after death?
What was his favourite *Carry On* film?
All said without pausing for breath

She asked about his health and wellbeing
Quizzed him on his current state of mind
Asked had he ever had his colon examined
And was he the marrying kind?

They just stared at each for a minute or more
Although it felt longer being conversationally bereft
Before she cracked a half smile in his general direction
Picked up her pork scratchings and left

OTHERWISE ENGAGED

I think it was morning – or afternoon
Although it could've been most of the day
I wasn't really watching the clock at the time
Otherwise engaged it's fair to say

I was abducted by gorgeous female aliens
To replenish their failing gene pool
All of them blonde with luscious lips and four breasts
And uniformly dressed by St.Trinian's School

I was mercilessly ravaged to within an inch of my life
And then again to within a quarter of an inch
And after a couple of peeled grapes and a Player's
    Navy Cut
I was back in pole position thanks to a winch
A walking frame and a block and tackle
Dear friends once more unto the breach
And after another twenty laps of the gene pool
I lost the use of both legs and my speech

In the blink of an eye I was flying backwards
On a threadbare magic carpet park and ride
My tongue was tied around no known language
And both eyes were wide shut and sun-dried

I felt hot and cold, sweet and sour
My landing gear was ripped and torn
Both ears were ravaged by headache
And I threw up another technicolor yawn

I struggled to focus, lost my sense of smell
Had a nark with my own reflection
The Martian nymphets were nowhere to be seen
I was broken and scarred by rejection

But now I've warmed to the cold light of day
And I've managed some joined-up thinking
It might be I wasn't really abducted at all
It was probably just the drinking

DENNIS

Dennis didn't really do that much
It's more than fair to say
Bugger all at weekends
Less on a weekday

He just sat there in the window
Watching the world go by
Perfecting the art of doing bugger all
Not even an occasional sigh

He didn't growl or bark or lick your face
Showed no interest in the postman's leg
Didn't do chewing slippers or chasing his tail
Let alone sit up and beg

Walkies didn't really do it for him
Neither did the latest squeaky toy
He never sank his teeth into a chew stick
Or curl his lip at the paperboy

He never even bothered to give your leg the eye
And playing ball was a definite no-no
As was lying down, sitting, staying and fetching
Even the bum across the carpet failed to show

So the veterinary surgeon was called to take a look
And the whole thing was brought to a head
After five hundred quid had greased the vet's palm
It turned out Dennis was dead

PROCLAMATION

He never said a word in the morning
Never chewed the fat late at night
His thoughts were never put into words of any kind
The gas and gab failed to ignite

He remained tight-lipped in conversation
Never once put his feelings into words
Said nothing at all about this or that
Or the other with the bees and the birds

He didn't do idle chatter
Never bothered to call her bluff
Spoke not once of speakable things
Or any other ordinary stuff

Didn't exchange any pleasantries
Or experiment with polite remarks
The purposeful adjective never showed its face
Idle chatter never showed its arse

He never poured out his true feelings
Never even gave vent to his spleen
Didn't partake in articulation
Left questions to die at the scene

He never indicated or suggested
Declared, emanated or muttered
Pronounced, suggested, transmitted or spilled
Spat out, mumbled or uttered
A single word of significance
A sentence or phrase great or small
So she left him for Jeffrey the speech therapist
In conclusion that says it all

I PREDICT A FRY UP

Oh the weeping and the torture
Now that she has gone
There's a hole in my life
I know she was the one

Bright-eyed and double gorgeous
Warm as an athlete's sock
Raven tresses, cheeky dresses
And a smile that could stop a clock

I remember the day like it was yesterday
Although I think it was two weeks last Sunday
We went out with a special Two-For-One voucher
That was only valid every other Monday

At a table for two in the window
We gazed into each other's eyes
Sipped cold tea from a runcible spoon
Then Googled 'runcible' eight or nine times

As she offered me the egg from her gammon
She mayonnaised most of her sleeve
Pepper-sneezed her bangers into her lap
And the fried bread decided to leave

Down the front stairs of her cleavage
With her plate spinning act in the air
The mushrooms stuck to her earlobes
Hash browns and beans in her hair

Tomato sauce ran from her nose
Black pudding shaded her eyes
She coughed and slipped on some peas on the floor
Spilling unsweetened tea on her thighs

She was now dressed in all day breakfast
I'd never seen her looking better
So I did what any hung over gentleman would do
I picked her up and I ate her

COMPRESSED AIR ON A G STRING

She was hotter than a pair of hot pants
That had been stuck behind a radiator for weeks
Hand made from extra strong gorgeousness
Wrapped in the unshabbiest of chic

We ran barefoot through the cornfields
Splashed red paint all over town
Gave it large, plenty, loads and more
Bigged it up, drank it in and played it down

Her magnetism tore at the rivets in my genes
Took aim and twice pulled the trigger
I loved her with all of my arse – I would've said heart
But obviously my arse is bigger

We got lost inside each others vests
Waylaid in an unmade bed
I thought she was more than the one for me
But it seems it was all in my head

Suddenly things became different
My slacks entered a state of flux
Everything I did and said only inflamed
Her allergy to laughter and hugs

The how's your father, monkey business, euphoria
 and stuff
Had packed up its belongings and gone
I was left feeling more like a number two
Than a prospective number one

She became distant with active indifference
And in what seemed like no time at all
I was down on the canvas and counted out
My belongings bin-bagged in the hall

I'd lost all sense of loved-upness
Capitulated in the face of desire
Been on the wrong side of one sidedness
And fell headlong into the fire
Of binned offness and rejection
Hopelessness and despair
And just to add insult to injury
She burst my inflatable chair

She said she couldn't stand it – it reminded her of me
Out of shape, full of wind and unhip,
Battered, transparent with a sticking plastered
bottom and often found in a skip

There was no need for that.

SHAMPOO SUPERNOVA

She said he was handsome
Intelligent, articulate and suave
A modern man who baked his own bread
Polite, kind and courteous
The perfect heir apparent
But there was no hair apparent on his head

He was challenged by follicles
A natural eggshell blond
But he did have a lovely head of skin
A virtual comb and brush set
Made of stainless style
And a head case to keep them in

He could look like a deodorant
In a turtle neck sweater
But he had this dapper style all of his own
And for emotional support
He had an iTunes Afro download
With the scalp application on his phone

And then one day in May
He came home and found the note

She'd be waving him goodbye first thing tomorrow
She'd been seeing someone else
With a fulsome head of hair
Parting can bring such sweet sorrow

FIBS

All women are fibbers, they bend the truth
They believe they're infallible and bullet proof
Their hearts are forged from case hardened steel
Their grasp of reality is beyond surreal

They cough on your dreams and vandalise your soul
Smash your loving cup with the remote control
They rearrange every minute of your waking hours
Can't see the beauty in garage forecourt flowers

They like to run your life on panic and disorder
Tackle a minor tiff with a Restraining Order
They're experts in semi-armed non-verbal combat
And they're always on a diet and always just as fat

They talk and talk and talk and talk and although
    talk is cheap
It's you who pays for all the words every single week
They say one thing and then they do another
Won't admit they're slowly turning into their mother
I mentioned these things to my true love
Accidentally while talking in my sleep
But despite one hand on the warming pan

And a slightly better physique
I'm writing this from Casualty
Mentally and physically scarred
While the hospital chaplain unravels my trousers
In search of my Donor Card

MOON FACE

Let's say goodnight
And switch off your light
Leave your fingerprints on the sky
Each and every night

Mr Man In The Moon
With your smiling round face
You look like Bobby Charlton
With a bit more pace

BULLET POINTS

Maybe it's a craving for acceptance
An emotional desire to belong
The need for a greater sense of identity
Or the peer pressure thing's far too strong

A lack of self-esteem and education
An absence of affection in their lives
Family breakdown, little money, fear of isolation
Perhaps the lust for power and status it satisfies

Look out for a change in appearance
An obsession with a clothing colour or style
An increased use of indecipherable slang
And a loss of the ability to smile

Then there's lying, stealing
Bullying, dealing
Robbery, thuggery
Forgery, muggery
Non-compliance
Aggressive defiance
Sexual innuendo
With an electrical appliance

Drug possession
A money obsession
Criminal damage
Violent aggression

The latest phones and designer clothes
Without explanation or compromise
There may be diamonds in the teeth
But there's nothing in the eyes

It'll never happen to us – that's what we say
In this world of gangs, guns and knives
That's something you read of in newspapers
That wrecks other peoples' lives

But never, ever be complacent
Darkness can emerge from brilliant light
You should never lose sight of this simple question
Do you know where your parents are tonight?

THE ART OF SEDUCTION

She was beautifully arranged on a stool at the bar
When I helped her with the lid on the pickled onion jar
Opening jars are mens work so it was done effortlessly
While giving the impression that she'd loosened it for me

After four and a half smiles, a couple of nods and a wink
She finally got her purse out and bought me a drink
We spoke about power tools, kids that give you lip
Doing proper slide tackles and going to the tip
Bar billiards, expensive chisels, paper aeroplanes
Insurance plans for hypertension, varicose veins
Noises that worry you, smells that make you faint
That thin bit of wood in the shed to stir paint

At this point two pickled eggs were added to the mix
With four tequila slammers and another onion fix
She pulled me close like a lamb bhuna to the slaughter
Although by now her breath was making my eyes water

I was completely under her influence, her control, her spell
Fully prepared to pucker up despite the awful smell

And as she whispered sweet somethings in my
    general direction
My crimplene trouser region sensed a real connection

Her mouth said I was gorgeous, her eyes said come to bed
Three bangers and a catherine wheel exploded in my head
We gazed into each other's eyes across the peanut bowl
I wondered if her sum parts were bigger than the whole

She pulled me towards her, I could feel the tension rise
I seductively puckered up and slowly closed my eyes
And woke up in an ambulance, my nose scrambled
    and runny
She'd butted me, knocked me out and stolen all my money

FRENZY

The word on the street was murder
A girl with helium implants
Was found slumped in chair with a mendacious smear
Down the back of her lounge suit pants

When the police arrived at the maisonette
They were appalled and shocked at the sight
Eyes widened and stomachs churned
As they scratched and sniffed through the night

The victim was covered in Tiramisu
She had an ear full of Spotted Dick
Gooey Fudge Brownies hung from her nose
And at least three coppers were sick

Apple Crumble, Cheesecake
Treacle Tarts, Clotted Cream
Evidence of Upside-Down-Cake
All present at the scene

Strawberry Shortcake, Banoffee Pavlova
Butterscotch Angel Delight
Gooseberry Fool and Sticky Toffee Pudding
But no sign of a struggle or fight

Finger prints and footprints
In Lemon Meringue Pie
Custard-stained serving spoons
And blueberry pie in the sky

This was indeed an unsavoury crime
But not murderous or perverted
She hadn't been killed to death at all
She'd simply been desserted

STARK

The biscuit barrel lies empty
The cupboard is practically bare
The kitchen bin remains full to the brim
And the Hoover in need of repair

The light in the fridge went out again
And hasn't even bothered to phone
The washing machine has refused to come clean
And the tin opener's accident prone

There's no fresh fruit in the fruit bowl
No blooming flowers in the hall
The ironing board has been put to the sword
And there's not even a helpline to call

Things aren't quite as I thought they'd be
And one thing in particular is clear
I'm so miserable without you
It's almost like you're still here

ROBERTA

Nobody had spoken of Auntie Roberta
Since the incident with the lawn mower mechanic
A deep and feeling heart and a generous mind
She could summon up and instigate panic
At the drop of a hat, in the wink of an eye
With a flick of her first and second fingers
She lived on brown ale, turnips and raisins
And could blow off some fearsome humdingers

She went to the dogs three times a week
Wore a 2HB pencil moustache
Smoked forty untipped cigarettes a day
Paid her dues in full and in cash

She swapped her court shoes for a sensible brogue
Had her undercarriage refurbished and redone
Progressed from she to he without passing go
And Bob's your uncle – job done

RAG

You can wear your gloves on the wrong feet
Expose your vajazzle in the middle of the street
Feed your addiction to soaps and cake
Throw all my Zappa records in the boating lake

Spend eight days a week bladdered on the lash
Kiss a female traffic warden on the moustache
Play the same song on the jukebox fifty times
Pull the head off my cuckoo every time the clock chimes

You can stump out your fags on the back of my head
Paint the whole house pink and the whole town red
You can smoke like a chimney, swear like a trooper
Feed me Maltesers with a pooper scooper

Pick other people's noses, throw my banjo out
Tell the window cleaner he's in with a shout
Go through my pockets three times every day
And I'll try and pay attention to every word you say

You can buy more shoes and handbags, sell my guitars
Ask random strangers in the street what gender they are

You can use more luxury bog roll than you normally do
Buy another chihuahua and another shiatsu

You can exaggerate another thirty seven million times
I'll overlook your flatulence and constant fashion crimes
You can do whatever you want to do when all is said
    and donc
Just never, never, ever, ever buy *The* f****** *Sun*

7 AM

I'm not at all keen on 7am
It's well past far too early for me
I have lie-down rows with alarm clocks
I get demoralised by breakfast TV

I'm short on mental ammunition
At this ungodly hour of the day
And wrapped in stains and aches and pains
Only adds to the sense of disarray
That kicks in when your head's full of headache
Hanging over from the night before
It's hard to think about the stuff in the sink
Or why the hell your trouser region is so sore

I'm a man of propensity and innate inclination
Disinclined to disposition or predilection
But I'm inclined to reconnect with my masculine side
If someone challenges a deep-rooted affection
Which is roughly what happened just hours ago
That's why I'm uncomfortable and can't sleep
It's all flooding back now on a tidal wave of nausea
If I wasn't so terribly unmanly I could weep

He walked into the restaurant and I caught his eye
Not the lazy one, the roving one of the two
The one that wanders aimlessly without destination
The one that's always shaded black and blue

I put my coat on and took my coat off
As the brandy on my steak was set aflame
He put his glasses on and took his glasses off
But the smoke blew up his chimney just the same

I looked at him and he looked at me
So I looked back at him a bit more
He looked at me again while I wasn't looking
And I thought 'sod it' and knocked him sparko on
the floor

He was smothered in Merlot and peppercorn sauce
With his tenderloin steak wrapped round his head
But old four eyes here had run off with my girl
So I think he had it coming – enough said

I was bounced from my table
And bounced out the door
Bounced off the parking meters
And bounced off the floor

She'll hate me more than ever now
That's it, that's the end, that's that
So never hit a man with glasses
Hit him with a baseball bat

AS YOU WERE

If I could speak to you
Just one more time
Instead of a ringing tone

I'd tell you
You're the best party
I've never thrown

BUTTERFLIES

Have you ever met someone
And felt a deep sense of connection?
A meeting of the mind, heart and soul
That makes the pulse race with affection?
You ache to spend every single minute together
To unfurl each others' wings, hold hands and fly
Up beyond the clouds to where the angels play
No – neither have I

THIS, THAT and the OTHER

Proclaim, circulate, announce and disclose
Be clear, concise and to the point
Open up, ventilate, get it off your chest
Spit it out and don't disappoint

Show off that special, God-given gift
For those fascinating topics of conversation
Share your razor-sharp wit and intelligence
And the low down on your latest crustacean

Discuss this and that and preferably the other
Don't fret over structure and grammar
But talk of diarrhoea and bodily functions
In a graceful and pleasing manner

Divulge your thoughts on football and shovels
Reveal where you stand on mood swings
The cult of celebrity, erectile dysfunction
And assorted other interesting things

Take a deep breath, slow down, sing out
Leave nothing of any interest unsaid
Project, enunciate, speak clearly and speak up
Or the art of eavesdropping is dead

AS IF

If you can be the sole of discretion
As honest as the day is long
Optimistic with a great sense of humour
Lavishly upholstered and strong

If you're riddled with love and affection
Erudite, eloquent and calm
Unshakably faithful with a loyalty card
Not averse to the taste of lip balm

If you can be financially responsible
Despite your interest in shoes
Hold a deep dislike of pork scratchings
Any televised sport and cheap booze

If you can route plan better than a sat nav
Can't leave your eyebrows alone
Reliable, committed, and scrupulously clean
With a distinct inability to moan

If you can be forgiving and respectful
Never make smells or snore
Remain sensitive, loving and deeply romantic
And can argue through a closed toilet door

If you're never wrong and always right
And never short tempered or late
You'll be more than just a top bloke
You'll be a woman, mate

MIDDAY

Lying here in bed thinking of all the mistakes I've made
The people I've hurt and disappointed
Relationships lost and mislaid

Things I really should've done and things I
    should've said
It really makes you stop and think
Have I got enough milk and bread?

OOLONG TEA and a GARIBALDI

She sipped from a cup of oolong tea
Her cheeks all flushed and sunken
Cracked a garibaldi with the sole of her shoe
Her preferred preparation for dunking

With lips pursed and eyes akimbo
She submerged the garibaldi in the plunge pot
But failed to withdraw before the crucial plop point
And lost the biscuit along with the plot

With a lapful of crumbs and dunk juice stains
She drooled, gurned, slobbered, whistled and swore
And even without the usual fricative consonant sounds
Her profanity-laced tirade was still hardcore

A lone she-wolf in sheep's clothing
Her day had gone from bad to even worse
And the empty glass at her bedside
Convinced her this was some kind of curse

She'd looked everywhere twice at least three times
Left no floorboard or flagstone unturned
And to make things worse her masticatory efficiency
Was now more than a case for concern

She couldn't eat or drink or enunciate
Let alone attempt a half decent pout
This crumbly catastrophe was just the last straw
What could she do save scream and shout?

So where had they gone? Where could they be?
She'd only last night wined and dined them
Little Bo Peep has lost her teeth
And doesn't know where to find them

LET'S TALK ABOUT ME

Some say irresponsible
Some say devil-may-care
Some say rude, off-hand and aggressive
A complete nightmare

Some say good for nothing
Some say ineffectual
Idle, worthless – a ne'er do well
A poorly dressed transsexual

A derelict, no good slacker
A loafer without means of support
An improvident, malingering wastrel
With a propensity to dance and cavort

Useless, incapable, and worthless
Can't work a washing machine
Appalling, unwholesome and despicable
With dubious personal hygiene

Some say unattractive
Distasteful and lacking in charm
Some say uneasy on the eye
As interesting as a burglar alarm

Some say untrustworthy
A shallow and dishonest wannabe
But that's more than enough about you dear
Let's talk about me

VALEDICTION

Discarded, disengaged, far flung, cast aside
Abandoned, binned and forsaken
Dumped, disentangled, junked, thrown over
Defriended, unpoked, stirred and shaken

You said you needed time on your own
To decide what you should do next
In less than ten minutes it'd all been thought through
You said it all in a two word text

Short, sharp, straight to the point
I know when to take a hint
But I couldn't help thinking how different it
could've been
If you weren't so ugly and skint

FRANK

Frank was an agitated, emotional wreck
Lonely, tired and overweight
He had a mood swing in the back garden
And a playhouse to procrastinate

His judgment was poor, he drank too much
He'd sleepwalk through his own snoring
So yoga was prescribed but to be perfectly frank
He found coping with stress was less boring

LAMINATE FLAW

She burst into the room during *Match of the Day*
Wearing a strongman's red wine moustache
Gave me both barrels shot straight from the lip
Brazen-faced, audacious and brash

She opened up with the toilet seat
And how I never replace toilet rolls
The ever present crumbs in the kitchen
And the collection of remote controls
My annoying inability to listen
The aversion to the vacuum cleaner
My active disinterest in handbags and shoes
And the bathroom floor misdemeanour

She said I'd no idea how to fold a towel
Called me thoughtless, insensitive and detached
Said I always parked the car in far flung spaces
So the bloody thing wouldn't get scratched

She hated my reluctance to acknowledge the
colour beige
And my pathetic martyr complex when I'm ill
(whaaat?!!)

Couldn't stand the empty ham packets in the fridge
Or the fact I'd never used her power drill

She kicked the pouffe as she left the room
It skidded across the laminate floor
The one I'd just stained with a double rum
    and coke
The one she'd finished laying the day before

I knew everything she'd thrown at me was
    probably true
And it's immature and churlish to avenge
But you should never go to bed on an argument
So I stayed awake to plot my revenge

MY BRILLIANT CAREER

It's underneath the orthopaedic mattress
Curled up inside at least three pairs of socks
In the freezer with the processed peas and carrots
Under the floorboards inside two broken clocks

It's tucked inside Fred Bear the threadbare teddy
Buried near the weeping willow tree
Jammed inside the reproduction fireplace
And best of all it all belongs to me

The dosh, the moolah, the bread, the wedge
The wonga, the readies, the cash
That gaggle of brown drinking vouchers
That makes up one's life savings stash

Monies from the string of hit singles
Royalties from stage and screen
Television, voice-overs and session fees
For vibraphone and mean tambourine

The gift that keeps on giving from the book sales
The film rights advance for Chapter One
The hatfuls of shrapnel from all night busking
As a gigolo from a time once upon

I've done the maths on the back of a beer mat
And the total sum is more than tidy
I've got enough to live comfortably for the
rest of my life
If I die a week on Friday

DINNER PARTY

A Thai green chicken curry dinner party banquet
Is simple for a man to prepare alone
You'll need two things to make this dish
A takeaway menu and a phone

HEADWAY

Pop out for a loaf or a pint of milk
Walk like a running man possessed
Liberally anoint yourself in anonymity
Wear a smile, wear a beard, wear a dress

Use all of your head to make headway
Adjourn the return to sender
Fare dodge, couch surf, live in a tent
If it works, change your name to Brenda

Steal a three-wheeler bicycle
Stow away on a cross channel ferry
Hide yourself deep in lost luggage
Tweet, think and be merry

Adopt a minimalist wardrobe
Rent everything rather than buy
Swap an arm and a leg off your overcoat
For a route map and a wave goodbye

Roller skate the edge of never
Race from here to nearly there
Join the Salvation Army, fake your own death
Fly like a bird through cleaner air

Save the Hitchhiker's Guide to the Fallacy
Re-make, re-model and rediscover
There's less to this than meets the eye
Nifty ways to leave your lover

THE TOBACCO PIRATES

Captain Bagwash was deaf in one earring
And wouldn't hear a word said against him
Furthermore, with his stumped out leg
It was unlikely he would stand for it either

He had a nicotine patch over one eye
This Jolly Jack low to middle tar
His filter was tipped and his shag ready rubbed
And his hornpipe could be seen from afar

With an uncorked bung-hole awash with booty
There was no greater Gentleman O'Fortune
He'd take out the Duke of Marlborough Light
And inhale the subtle aroma and perfume

He was spliced with Golden Virginia
A wench who rolled her own gaspers
She had a smoker's cough on a dead man's chest
And a bilge rat trapped in her jaspers

They plundered away in parrot fashion
All leeward and capstan full strength
Hip deep in heave-ho and barbarity
Smoking kippers at arms length

But just one drag can blow the man down
And Grace O'Malley stumped out her butt
Set Bagwash alight with dark rum and desire
Sweeping him right off his foot

In no time she'd lowered his colours
Had five of his his pieces of eight
Ahoy, aloft, amidships and avast
Causing his pantaloons to inflate

This sparked up a front-loaded Virginia
Who flew into O'Malley's face
Unleashing a rage from the jaws of hell
Skin and hair all over the place

She then turned her attention to Bagwash
Soaked him right through from the deep
And plugged him into the Spanish mains
Making even the hardiest souls weep

Smoke rings danced from his earholes
Scorch marks appeared on his shirt
The gift of ignition kept on giving
And nostrils were offended and hurt

His eyes rolled, lit up and smouldered
His doubloons burst into flames
Smokestack lightening shot up his breeches
Until only his eye teeth remained

Virginia stood over his dentures
And kicked them over the side
Down into Davy Jones' locker
Where the souls of dead men lie

She smiled and lit up a rollie
But the match fell free from her grip
Down into her lap near her gunpowder plot
And blew up the whole bleeding ship

WARNING : SMOKING KILLS

KEEPS

You can keep the TV aerial
The kettle and frying pan
I'm not that bothered about the shower curtain
Or the bathroom extractor fan

You can hang on to the tin opener
And the salt and pepper shakers
The door handles, light bulbs
Coffee and smoothie makers
The Ali Baba laundry basket
Fridge freezer and microwave
The smoke detector, stepladder
My records and aftershave

Keep hold of the cheese and vegetable grater
The hearth rug and the fuse box
The Yorkshire stone fireplace
And all my shoes and socks

It's not the stuff that I'm missing
I don't care about those things
There's nothing more important than relationships
And now my heart no longer sings

I'm begging you to reconsider
Now you're out kissing frogs
I've never been so lonely since you left
So for God's sake bring back the dog

CAREFUL IN THOSE SLACKS EUGENE

When green is no longer flavour of the month
And blackberries ripen on the bough
Autumn unfurls its middle finger at the sun
Ploughing furrows deep into the brow

I turn to face myself again and promise that I shan't
Risk even half an eye but somehow I can't
Resist a fleeting glance before a rising sense of dread
Is shimmying and sequinned, legs-a-kimbo in my head

There's a call to arms and a call to legs
An oiling of the parts that are rusting
Geezers with blisters and Chubby Checker twisters
Flaunting, haunting and thrusting

The tentative first step, two-step doorstep
A willingness to funk your strutting stuff

Drain pipe dreams bursting at the seams
And those looking in can't get enough

Of the elegant and floaty, flatulent and bloaty
Fresh-faced, well-worn and comic

Splintered floorboards, bum notes and dischord
Underdone, over-ripe and atomic

Arses for courses, donkeys and horses
That lift, fall, slip, maul and drop

Gallopers, trippers, lollopers and slippers
Wrapped in static, crackle and pop

Slim girls with wide boys, merrymakers, killjoys
Dressing up before the dressing down

Clumsiness and grace, a fumbled embrace
And more body talk of the town

Fluency, poise
Momentary joys
Positional scuffles
Soft shoe shuffles
Inelegance and stiffness
Exposed midriffness
Awkwardness, gracefulness
Sugared up tastefulness
Refinement, poise
Tranquility and noise

Shockers, knockers
Beta blockers
Bodily disfunctions
Wardrobe malfunctions
Decorum, finesse
That dress and distress

It's the razzle-dazzled twinkle-toed three left feet
That beckons you seductively back into your seat
It's not the skimpies, flesh and legs, it's the
    diamante romancing
That's why loads of blokes watch *Strictly Come
    Dancing*

I've not seen it myself.

THE COST OF LOVING

I needed to talk to her, to explain the situation
In the faint hope she'd understand
How things can be blown out of all proportion
And rapidly get out of hand

So from the 11.48 train to Euston
I called her at work and got the switchboard
But as you never get to speak to a human these days
I was quickly put to the sword

To the tune of Handel's *Water Music*
I waited patiently for a reply
Stained the train window
With a cough and another sigh
Counted eighty seven sheep
Two postmen and a goat
And as Handel was substituted by Billy Joel
The recorded messenger cleared its throat

> 'Take two steps back from the window
> Shuffle three feet to the left
> Sit down and press 1 repeatedly
> When prompted, hold your breath.

Smile and press your trousers
Bristle while you wait
Don't say or press anything else
When pressed for an answer press 8.
Take off your shirt
Put your phone voice on
Quote your house number and postcode
Quote from the Bible
Quote Shakespeare and Lennon
Then quote for resurfacing the road.
Put your left leg in, put your records on
Press 7 for the full nine yards
At the next prompt press 3 then 4 then 5
Or press 12 for a game of cards.
Press wild flowers, press release
Press up against the table
Press # then * for the default menu
Press 999 if unstable.
Put your best face forward
Put your lighter in the air
Put your iPod on shuffle
Put your watch in for repair.
We're trying to connect you
Trying to resurrect you
We're trying for a baby
Trying to redirect you......'

Although I had risen to 43rd in the queue
I knew there was no way back
When, like me, the battery on my mobile
Lost its spark, threw in its hand and went flat

I needed to talk to her and explain the situation
To point out that I'm suffering from stress
But now she'll go home and confront my indiscretion
And I'll probably have to change my address

The last time it happened – it has happened before
She poured paint stripper over my car
Cleaned the toilet rim with my toothbrush
Filled my shoes with boiling hot tar
Cut up all the clothes in my wardrobe
Set fire to my banjo collection
Instigated rumours of raging STDs
And played havoc with my rhythm section

I know I've been stupid
And I need to wise up
But like most men I'm not immune to these sins
But at the end of the day
All I wanted to say
Was I'd forgotten to take out the bins

The 'L' Word

Is it some sort of temporary madness?
A celestial gift from above?
It thrills and kills indiscriminately
What is this thing called love?

A desire that burns and makes pulses race
A mouth full of unquotable quotes
Butterflies that feel like acrobats
In powdered glass overcoats

I've been known to baulk at the merest hint
Of the 'L' word – this much is true
But my stomach's been churning and it's not
indigestion
The cause of it all could be you

I'm repressing my feelings and sensitive leanings
It's only what most blokes would do
But let's get this straight, you can't deny fate
We were made for each other, me and you

I could be the face that takes the place of what's his face
You know, that ginger haired fella you've just binned

And with this feverish excitement and
    simmering lust
I could be the wings beneath your wind

The full fat cheese to your low fat crackers
The innersole mate for your dancing shoes
The open arms on your favourite jacket
The laser for your 'love' and 'hate' tattoos
I could be the sour cream on your fajita
The novelty umbrella each time it rains
The on and off knob on your convector heater
The punch bag during period pains

I could wake you each morning with breakfast in bed
Make you laugh on the hour every hour
Massage your ego, your feet and your head
And clean the lime scale off the tiles in the shower

With my love of Drambuie
And extreme tonsil tennis
I could live with your Tourette's
And surly menace
What a wonderful life
We could share you and me
If only you weren't the psychiatrist
That sectioned me

NEVILLE FLOWERS IS A VERY NICE MAN

Back in the day when they danced to The Kinks
And every TV drama featured kitchen sinks
The Flowers, they were blooming and their love
    was true
And the world had never even heard of B&Q

But it wasn't too long before the rot set in
And although it wasn't what you'd call a cardinal sin
She didn't mind the beer and she could tolerate
    the fags
But she couldn't stand his stash of DIY mags

Hand tools, Cuprinol
Wood glue, spag bol
Ginger nuts, bib and brace
Half price fireplace
Rusty hinge, multi-tool
Turks head, steel rule
Swarfiga, wood screw
Wing nut, Love Me Do

She ate a Toblerone down the telephone
When she finally told him she was leaving home

It floored him like the decking on his new veranda
So he tried to smooth it over with a Black &
Decker sander

But she was having none of it and told him the score
He tried to entice her with a woodblock floor
Some Rapid Hardware vouchers, beads and bangles
But where she walked with angels, he worked
with angles

Hand tools, Cuprinol
Wood glue, spag bol
Ginger nuts, bib and brace
Half price fireplace
Rusty hinge, multi-tool
Turks head, steel rule
Swarfiga, wood screw
Wing nut, Love Me Do

He misses her touch when he unblocks a drain
(She was decorated for bravery in the bathroom
campaign)
The Celtic tattoo on her left bingo wing
And the way she blew smoke through her
sovereign ring

Now he whiles away the hours in the downstairs bog
Fingering the pages of the Argos catalogue
And fondly remembers the power drill he lent her
When he dines alone at the Garden Centre

Even his best kecks are peppered with Artex
But Neville Flowers is a very nice man
He's bloody fantastic with sealant and mastic
Neville Flowers is a very nice man
B&Q, Home Base nonpartisan
Chandeliers in his caravan, man
Neville Flowers is a very nice man

FOREVER

I thought it was forever
Whatsername and me
We'd stay up late every night
Watching crap TV
Then one night she left me
Emotionally bereft
Now all I've got is bloodshot eyes
And no Maltesers left

LESSONS IN LOVE

When I stop to reflect and consider
I still struggle to make sense of it all
She talked very fast and listened very slow
As she packed up her bags in the hall

All attempts at reconciliation
Were unilaterally dismissed
She said the last thing she wanted was to hurt me
But it was still number three on the list
Which was more than disappointing
Given all that we'd been through
Since she first puckered up and threw the lips on me
In the summer of '92

I remember the first time I made her laugh
She farted and blew a snot bubble
Coffee streamed from her nostrils
And her bourbons were reduced to rubble
But after I'd sponged down her boob tube
And wiped most of her cough from my knee
I looked into her eyes of blue
And knew she was the girl for me

She was alive and drop-dead gorgeous, wrapped
in Hepburn chic
She was so bespoke whenever she spoke she
spoke in pure bespeak
Every moving part of her was made from extra
lovely things
She was more angel than Angel Delight – she
was only missing wings

She was the bread to my jam
I was the fritter to her spam
She was the hurly to my burly
I was the curly to her wurly
She was the whip to my lash
The bang and wallop to my crash
I was the singer to her thong
She was the ping to my pong

We'd seen so much together
Shared so many things
Earache, colds, bird 'flu, fleas
Trench foot and almost wedding rings

I couldn't let her walk away
I had to let her know

Just how much she meant to me
And let my feelings show
So I pulled myself together
Adopted a manly stance
And although I might have allowed my feminine side
To get in touch with my pants
I knew it was now or never
To open up and pour out my heart
Tell her all those things I should've said
And not let this tear us apart

So I told her we belonged together
And although the situation was tense
I explained my cost benefit analysis
And how it all made financial sense

She assaulted me with a sock puppet and a
billiard ball
I was in intensive care for over a week
But if nothing else she taught me something
money can't buy
Think before you speak

HEART.SONG

I'm not really sure
I don't really know
Which way to turn
Or which way to go

Even pick-me-ups
Pick me up and put me down
Smiles turn themselves
Upside down into a frown

I don't like going out
Can't stand staying in
Everything's a ball ache
My head's in a constant spin

I'm not the man I used to be
Things have radically changed
My social circle's triangular
Since my flowers were rearranged

From cannonball to Malteser
From a Bigger Bang to a fart
I'd love to love someone to love
But I haven't got the heart

So I moan and groan and groan and moan
And that's it – my response
Although on the brighter side
I did win a book token once

UNSAID and DONE

In answer to the question
Allegorical and satirical
Rich man, beggar man, emotional thief
Old hat, new man, or miracle
The devil lies in the detail
When all's unsaid and done
Life's not an optical illusion
It just looks like one

CONUNDRUM

Awash with joy
Overcome with bliss
Butterflies flutter in the abdomen
At the thought of a solitary kiss

Oh to taste your sugared lips
Inhale your peroxide hair
I'd love to be your bicycle seat
Or the surgical ring on your chair

You're more than a storm in a D cup
More than a twinge down below
This thing's bigger than both of us
And I've been taking those pills as you know

It's a profound metaphysical conundrum
That's left me feeling this way
I'm in search of a story that just won't be found
If I'm honest in the cold light of day

But there's one thing I'd really like you to know
And it's endorsed by hard medical facts
I've only ever had eyes for you
I think I've got cataracts

REPEAT and FADE

Doo-Wah-Diddy-Doddy
Dum-Hidi-Hoo-Wah
Rizzle-Fiddle-Piggy-Middle
Zipper-Dee-Poo-Pah
Yes! Yes!
Yes! Yes!
Yes! Yes! Yes!

Rum-Bum-Doodle-Um
Lippy-Dippy-Um-Yah
Sticky-Foo-Chocky-Woo
Dippy-Trippy-Mars-Bar
Yes! Yes!
Yes! Yes!
Yes! Yes! Yes!

Tricky-Dicky-Doo-Dah
Diddle-Hum-Drum
Hiddy-Hoo-Hi-Di-Du
Oooh-Dicky-Di-Dum

Wham-Bam-Razzle-Flam
Score-Draw-Phwoar!
If this song was my girlfriend
I'd have listened to her more

FEMME FATALITY

With you I only wanted
A one life stand
With you I only wanted
A hold to hand

Isms became wasms
And I was the second to know
You were like an uncaught falling star
I just missed the end of the show

So I've written these few lines for you
Drawn from my own phrenology
With an imaginary musical accompaniment
Composed from notes of apology

With you I only wanted
A one life stand
With you I only wanted
A hold to hand

Not even a look, just a glimpse would do
Of the things I used to mean to you